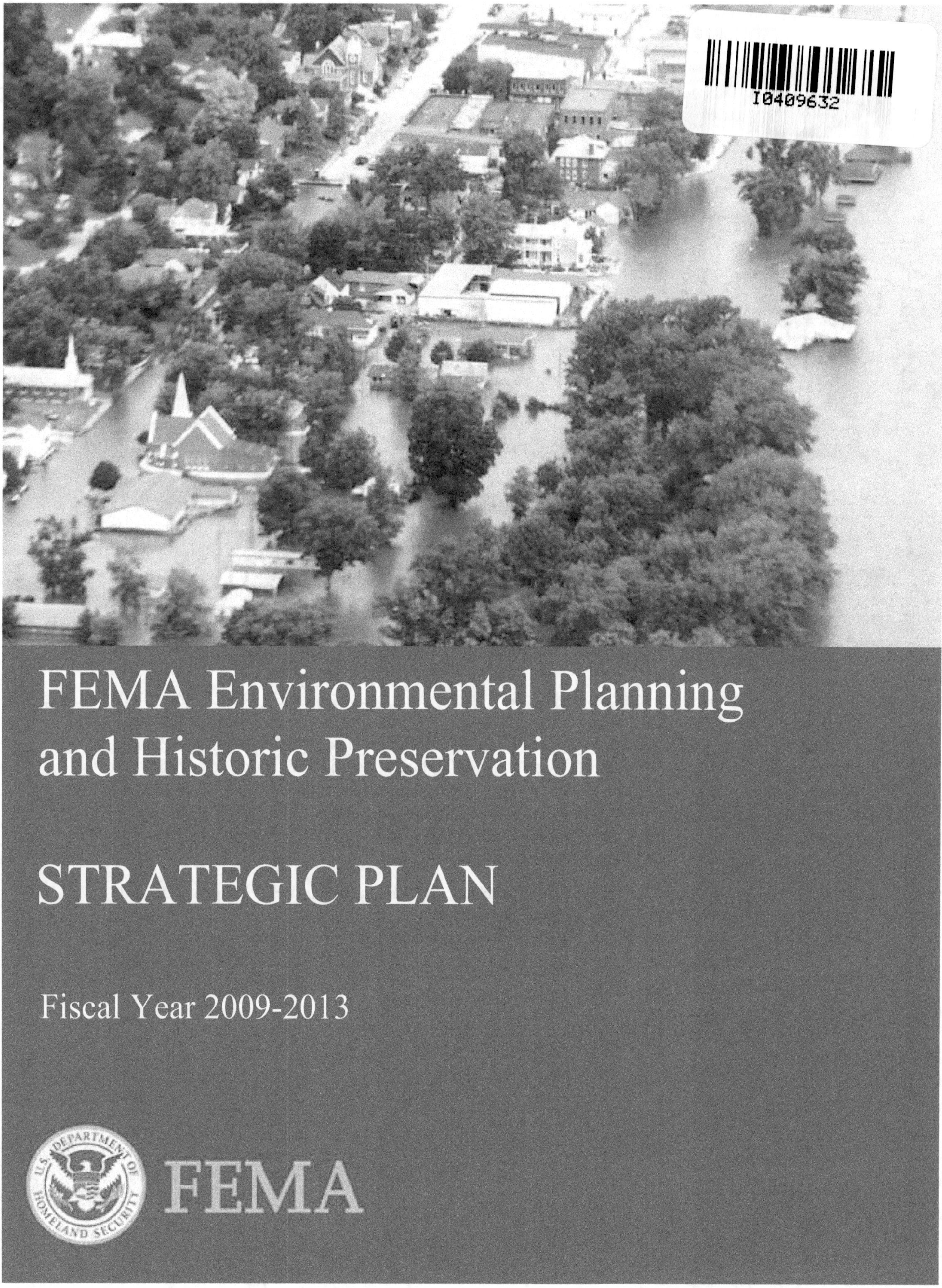

FEMA Environmental Planning and Historic Preservation

STRATEGIC PLAN

Fiscal Year 2009-2013

FEMA

Message from the Administrator

The Federal Emergency Management Agency (FEMA) believes environmental stewardship, historic preservation, and emergency management have complementary goals that, when considered together in a strategic manner, help to prevent or minimize the impacts of all hazards and restore and preserve the natural and cultural fabric of a community following a disaster.

The FEMA Environmental Planning and Historic Preservation (EHP) Strategic Plan for Fiscal Years 2009-2013 reflects the Agency's commitment to the strategic integration of EHP considerations into the implementation of its programs, policies and overall mission. The EHP Strategic Plan presents the goals, objectives and strategies that will guide and inform the evolution of FEMA's EHP operations.

This document is the culmination of an extensive planning effort led by FEMA's Office of Environmental Planning and Historic Preservation (OEHP) in collaboration with a Steering Committee composed of Headquarters and Regional program staff. Because OEHP assists all FEMA programs in ensuring compliance with federal EHP requirements, gaining program support for the Strategic Plan was a key priority in the development process. Although development of the Strategic Plan began in April 2008 with the intent of having it in place for FY 2009, several cycles of review and writing were necessary to ensure program buy-in before it was finalized in 2010.

It is a testament to the mutual commitment of Agency components to timely, reliable and efficient EHP compliance operations that several key priorities identified as a result of the strategic planning effort have already been accomplished in anticipation of the Strategic Plan's final approval. A few achievements I would like to highlight include: the completion of EHP Credentialing Plans, the placement of Deputy Regional Environmental Officers in all FEMA regions, the finalization of Executive Order 11988 training, the completion of draft revised environmental requirements and procedures, the completion of a draft of Executive Order 11988 Strategy, and the establishment of the EHP Advisory Committee.

The Steering Committee's dedication to a comprehensive and balanced EHP Strategic Plan and their efforts to engage all FEMA stakeholders in the Plan's development are greatly appreciated. We look forward to integrating the goals, objectives and strategies identified in this Plan into the Agency's EHP operations across all programs in support of the EHP, FEMA and Department of Homeland Security (DHS) mission.

W. Craig Fugate

Administrator

Table of Contents

Executive Summary

The Environmental Planning and Historic Preservation (EHP) Strategic Plan 2009-2013 is the result of an extensive planning process led by the Office of Environmental Planning & Historic Preservation (OEHP). This process included several rounds of vetting and writing in order to ensure maximum stakeholder input and buy-in.

The direction and impetus for the plan began at the Regional Environmental Officers (REO) meeting in November 2007. In April 2008, a Steering Committee helped identify five-year goals and objectives. In June 2008, a large number of internal Federal Emergency Management Agency (FEMA) stakeholders came together to validate the draft goals and objectives, develop supporting strategies, and sketch the plan's framework. The Steering Committee then edited this draft, and developed implementation plans to support the objectives and priority strategies. The plan has been vetted by FEMA program offices and the EHP Advisory Committee (EHPAC). The EHP Strategic Plan was approved on June 3, 2010.

The major themes that have significantly shaped FEMA's EHP Strategic Plan for 2009-2013 include: increased EHP capabilities both internal and external to FEMA; efficiencies gained through cross-program integration of EHP functions, technology, and processes; and increased EHP awareness that leads to better partnerships and action. The following goals and objectives represent the culmination of this work:

❖ **Goal 1: Build Sustainable Capabilities**
- **OBJECTIVE 1.1:** Strengthen EHP Human Capital.
- **OBJECTIVE 1.2:** Develop an investment and funding support strategy to meet FEMA's EHP compliance goals and program metrics.

❖ **Goal 2: Strengthen Operational Effectiveness**
- **OBJECTIVE 2.1:** Simplify, standardize and improve the EHP compliance process across all programs.
- **OBJECTIVE 2.2:** Integrate EHP requirements into program goals, development, implementation and performance
- **OBJECTIVE 2.3:** Leverage technology in the EHP compliance process.
- **OBJECTIVE 2.4:** Evaluate the reliability, consistency, cost effectiveness, and timeliness of EHP's compliance process.

❖ **Goal 3: Strengthen Partnerships**
- **OBJECTIVE 3.1:** Increase awareness of the value of the EHP compliance process across FEMA programs and among stakeholders, in order to foster a sense of ownership of and responsibility for EHP compliance.
- **OBJECTIVE 3.2:** Improve coordination with Resource Agencies.
- **OBJECTIVE 3.3:** Develop and implement EHP partnering opportunities to advance the FEMA mission.

The EHP Strategic Plan lays out a path for a robust EHP program that strengthens FEMA's programs and protects FEMA's investments.

Background

The Federal Emergency Management Agency (FEMA) is the Federal agency responsible for supporting our citizens and first responders to ensure that as a nation we work together to build, sustain, and improve our capability to prepare for, protect against, respond to, recover from, and mitigate all hazards. Environmental stewardship and historic preservation support emergency management goals and aid to prevent or minimize the impacts of these emergency situations/events. Protection and stewardship of the Nation's natural resources, landscapes, and cultural sites provides increased protection from disasters to communities throughout the country.

The Environmental Planning and Historic Preservation (EHP) Mission and "Value to Society"

The EHP function serves the Nation by ensuring that valuable natural and cultural resources are considered in all FEMA emergency management decisions and disaster operations.

The EHP requirements outlined in numerous laws, executive orders, and regulations were designed by Congress to inform and improve federal decision-making and use Federal agencies as examples for the stewardship of natural, cultural and historic resources. EHP requirements must be considered together with the operational nature of FEMA's mission, to ensure FEMA provides

"Agency managers who have learned to use [the National Environmental Policy Act] have discovered that it helps them do their jobs. It can make it easier to discourage poor proposals, reduce the amount of documentation down the road, and support innovation. NEPA helps managers make better decisions, produce better results, and build trust in surrounding communities. It makes good economic sense, and is, quite simply, good government."

~Council on Environmental Quality

THE NATIONAL ENVIRONMENTAL POLICY ACT: A Study of Its Effectiveness After Twenty-five Years, CEQ 1997

assistance in a timely, reliable and cost effective way.

The Office of Environmental Planning and Historic Preservation (OEHP) works with FEMA Program offices and disaster operations to ensure the EHP compliance process facilitates good decision-making.

This process, if done programmatically and proactively, can:

- Ensure effective and efficient delivery of FEMA's mission;
- Enable informed and transparent decision-making; and
- Reduce the negative impacts of disasters and emergency management decisions on the human environment through stewardship of natural, cultural and historic resources.

Organizational History

The EHP function within FEMA began with the development of environmental regulations in the late 1980s, and a surge in interest in both environmental and historic preservation issues and requirements as a result of a series of disasters in the late 1980s and early 1990s, including Hurricane Hugo in 1989, Hurricane Andrew in 1992, the Mid-west floods in 1993, and the Northridge Earthquake in 1994. At that time, environmental planning (led by an Environmental Officer) and historic preservation (led by a Federal Preservation Officer) were separate functions within FEMA and in separate organizations, ranging from the Office of the Administrator, the Office of Policy and Program Analysis, Office of Regional Operations, the Response and Recovery Directorate, and the Federal Insurance and Mitigation Administration.

The Headquarters environmental function expanded to the regions in 1996 with the creation of Regional Environmental Officers (REO). In 2003, the Environmental Planning and Historic Preservation functions were combined under the FEMA Mitigation Directorate (now Federal Insurance and Mitigation Administration). In 2006, EHP was established as a separate organization with dedicated EHP management for the first time. In 2008, recognizing the importance of the function to the successful implementation of FEMA's programs, it was established as an Office, becoming the Office of Environmental Planning & Historic Preservation (OEHP).

Today, OEHP is the functional leader within FEMA for the interpretation and consistent application of EHP requirements and the single source of cross-program EHP policy, guidance, training and systems within FEMA, recognized across Federal agencies for its innovation and flexibility in achieving EHP compliance.

Other environmental functions also exist within FEMA. After the creation of the Department of Homeland Security (DHS) in 2003, FEMA began to realize the scope of environmental management issues that had not been addressed in the past, and created an environmental management (EM) function within the facilities management organization and responsibilities. EHP and EM functions are complementary functions that achieve the environmental policy goals for the Agency and support the continuity of FEMA's operations. However, the environmental scope of the two functions significantly differ with respect to; legal obligations and their application relative to FEMA's responsibilities, operating conditions, and impacted stakeholders.

Achieving the EHP Mission

The mission and functions of EHP are carried out across FEMA, with distinct roles and responsibilities across OEHP, Regions, and Program proponents. The two major functions of OEHP are:

(1) <u>Functional EHP leadership & authority.</u> Working with DHS and outside Federal, State, Territorial and Tribal resource agencies and stakeholders, EHP develops and implements a compliance framework for FEMA, establishes a performance management system for EHP compliance within FEMA, and has delegated approval authority to make compliance determinations.

(2) <u>Policy and technical support.</u> OEHP provides general policy guidance on the integration of EHP compliance requirements across FEMA programs and works with the programs to ensure that the appropriate funding, systems and human capital are in place to support these requirements. OEHP provides the appropriate expertise to assist programs in the integration of these requirements into program processes and procedures.

A Dual Workforce

Program proponents, (those offices within FEMA that manage programs or are in the operational line of authority for FEMA actions), have the responsibility to ensure EHP compliance in programs and activities and provide appropriate resources to meet these needs.

OEHP consists of both a permanent workforce as well as an EHP disaster workforce.

- The permanent workforce is comprised of Headquarters OEHP staff (OEHP Director, Agency Federal Preservation Officer, Agency Environmental Officer, and support staff), and Regional OEHP staff (ten Regional Environmental Officers (REOs) and their support staff).
- The EHP cadre is made up of disaster reservists with the EHP expertise who provide support for disaster operations.

OEHP works and consults with many internal and external partners to consider environmental and historic impacts in the decision-making process.

Drivers of the Strategic Plan

In support of FEMA's mission to support our citizens and first responders to ensure that as a nation we work together to build, sustain, and improve our capability to prepare for, protect against, respond to, recover from, and mitigate all hazards, the Agency needed to evaluate its history in meeting its EHP responsibilities and determine the future direction necessary to support FEMA's programs. Over the past few years, there have been many drivers that necessitated the development of an EHP Strategic Plan.

Growth in FEMA

Over the years leading up to this strategic planning effort, there was extensive program growth across FEMA. This was in large part due to an increase in disaster declarations, including the extensive and complex EHP issues associated with Hurricane Katrina which significantly impacted the effectiveness of the EHP function (which had not grown since the late 1990s). In addition to the number of disasters, program growth included many new non-disaster grant programs, such as the Pre-Disaster Mitigation Program, Repetitive Flood Claims, and Severe Repetitive Loss, as well as the 2007 integration of approximately 20 National Preparedness Grant Programs. The EHP function had in the past been very focused on disaster operations, but these new programs demanded new approaches, as well as new resources to provide support. This growth also created a higher demand for cross-program policies, standardized systems, and general operational efficiencies. This added to an existing need to incorporate requirements from DHS management directives related to environmental planning and historic preservation into existing regulations, policies, procedures and guidance.

FEMA's Transformation

Transformation within FEMA, begun in the aftermath of Katrina, demanded that the EHP function take a strategic and holistic approach to meet operational needs and changes, and further aid in streamlining the grant award process. As a support function, this is impossible to accomplish without a solid understanding of our internal customers needs and priorities across FEMA. A strategic approach that included representatives from the various programs with EHP roles and responsibilities was the best way to tackle these issues. Process integration, improved partnerships and resource requirements were at the top of this list.

> **Steering Committee**
> ❖ Chair (Director OEHP)
> ❖ FEMA Headquarters
> – Federal Insurance and Mitigation Administration
> – Recovery Directorate
> – Grants Programs Directorate
> – Office of Management
> ❖ FEMA Regions (II, X)

Our Approach to Strategic Planning

Since EHP is an integrated function across FEMA programs, it is critical that those most affected by it are involved in identifying requirements for the most effective program delivery. Led by OEHP, a cross-functional Steering Committee was assembled in April 2008 which began the official process of identifying five-year goals and objectives. This Steering Committee included representation from regions, program offices, and OEHP staff.

- Before the Committee established the goals and objectives, they first fully clarified the EHP function's *value to society* and how it supported the FEMA mission. The effort to define EHP's value to society was the foundation for the plan. The Steering Committee then developed the first draft of EHP goals and objectives. These goals and objectives went through an internal vetting cycle across the programs and other key OEHP staff.

The timeline of strategic planning events included the following:

❖ **April 2008 – Strategic Planning Kick-Off** – The Strategic Plan Steering Committee defined EHP's value to society, drafted goals and objectives, and validated mission and vision.

❖ **June 2008 – Large Stakeholder Event** – A larger stakeholder event convened that included a wider array of participants in addition to the Steering Committee. In this event, stakeholders modified draft objectives and then detailed out the specific strategies, timelines and resources needed to achieve the objectives based on program needs.

❖ **July-August 2008 – Review Cycle and Writing** - After the stakeholder session, the strategies were put through an internal review cycle across the programs and assessed by other key OEHP staff. During this time, a first draft of the plan was written using the defined goals, objectives, and strategies.

❖ **August 2008 – Steering Committee Meeting** – The Steering Committee finalized the goals, objectives and strategies and identified a preliminary set of performance metrics to measure success. At the same time, they prioritized the strategies in the plan and developed preliminary implementation and funding plans associated with the strategies. The prioritized strategy implementation plans can be found in the (*Appendix C: Summary of Implementation Plans and Priority Strategies*, pg C-1).

❖ **September 2008 - November 2009 – Vetting Cycle and Final Modifications** - In the fall of 2008, the draft Strategic Plan was reviewed by OEHP HQ and regional staff, the Steering Committee, and Program Management. Finally, OEHP sent the plan for review by the FEMA Policy Working Group (PWG), and for briefing by the EHP Advisory Committee (EHPAC), before it was approved by the FEMA Administrator.

All strategies within this plan were developed with the clear understanding that alignment to FEMA Strategic Goals and Objectives is critical to the success of the Plan and the overall Mission of the Agency. In so doing, the EHP Strategic Plan supports the FEMA Strategic Plan and planning efforts within the DHS Office of Occupational Safety and Environmental Programs.(*Appendix B: Link to FEMA and DHS Strategic Plans/OEHP Performance Measures*).

The following actions conducted in FY2009 reflect the initial effort towards the implementation of this plan:

- Goal 1: Build Sustainable Capabilities
    - Secured funding for additional Deputy Regional Environmental Officers
    - Developed the EHP Credentialing Plan for the Disaster Workforce
- Goal 2: Strengthen Operational Effectiveness
    - Completed draft revision of FEMA environmental regulations (44 CFR Part 9)
    - Developed and began implementation of an EHP policy framework
    - Developed FEMA's E.O. 11988 Strategy (Floodplain Management)
- Goal 3: Strengthen Partnerships
    - Implemented an EHP Advisory Committee (EHPAC) at the national level

EHP Mission, Vision, Goals, and Objectives

FEMA's EHP Mission

Help communities reduce the impact that disasters and emergency management (preparedness, protection, response, recovery, and mitigation) decisions and operations have on the nation's natural and cultural resources.

Vision

FEMA actively strives to fulfill its mission in compliance with national environmental planning and historic preservation policies, through the full and transparent integration of EHP values and requirements into emergency management decision-making and processes.

FEMA EHP GOALS

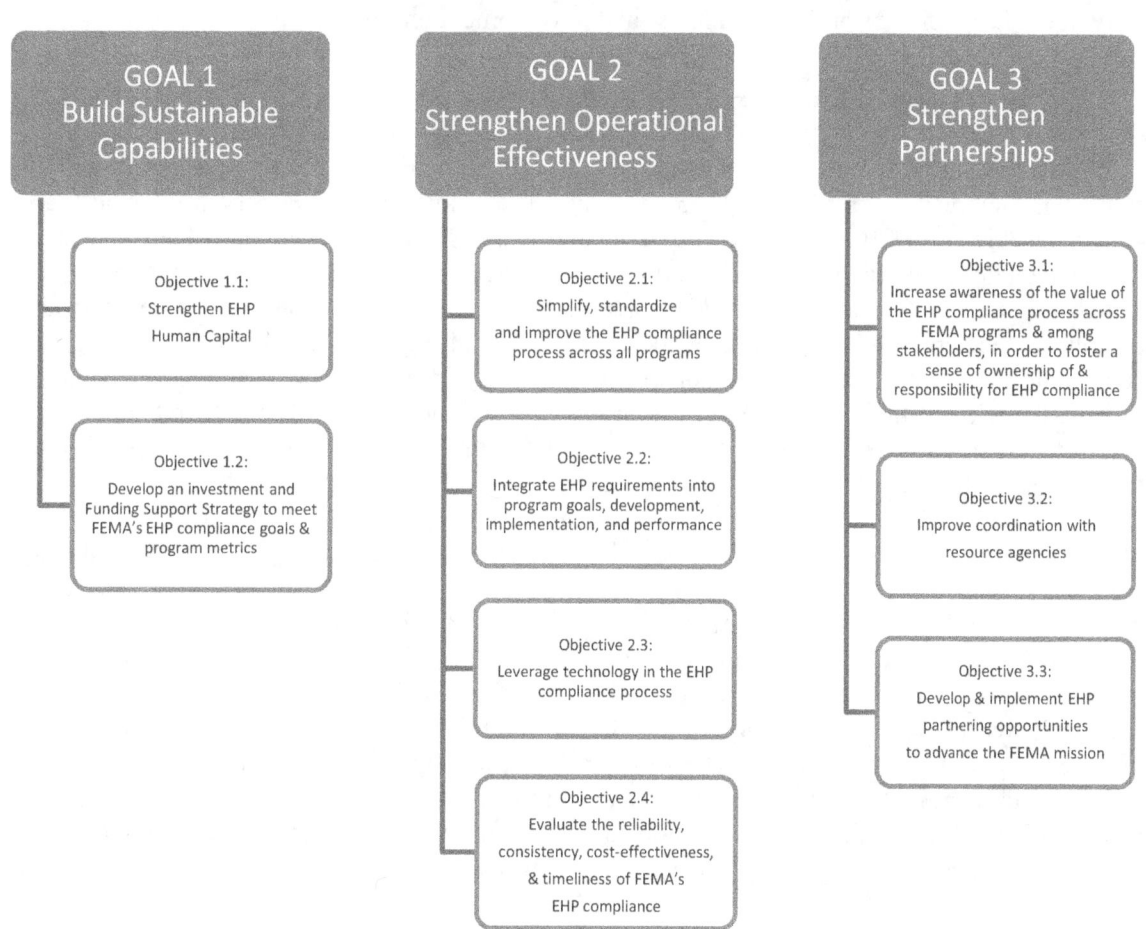

GOAL 1
Build Sustainable Capabilities

Objective 1.1:
Strengthen EHP Human Capital

Objective 1.2:
Develop an investment and Funding Support Strategy to meet FEMA's EHP compliance goals & program metrics

GOAL 2
Strengthen Operational Effectiveness

Objective 2.1:
Simplify, standardize and improve the EHP compliance process across all programs

Objective 2.2:
Integrate EHP requirements into program goals, development, implementation, and performance

Objective 2.3:
Leverage technology in the EHP compliance process

Objective 2.4:
Evaluate the reliability, consistency, cost-effectiveness, & timeliness of FEMA's EHP compliance

GOAL 3
Strengthen Partnerships

Objective 3.1:
Increase awareness of the value of the EHP compliance process across FEMA programs & among stakeholders, in order to foster a sense of ownership of & responsibility for EHP compliance

Objective 3.2:
Improve coordination with resource agencies

Objective 3.3:
Develop & implement EHP partnering opportunities to advance the FEMA mission

EHP Goals, Objectives, and Strategies

GOAL 1: BUILD SUSTAINABLE CAPABILITIES

The Federal Emergency Management Agency (FEMA) environmental planning and historic preservation (EHP) mission is successfully achieved by building and sustaining its capabilities and those of its partners for addressing compliance with the national EHP policies captured in multiple EHP-related laws, Presidential Executive Orders, and Regulations. The EHP function is supported by the Office of Environmental Planning and Historic Preservation (OEHP), which is comprised of staff at FEMA Headquarters; Regional Environmental Officers (REOs) and their Deputy Regional Environmental Officers (DREOs); and the EHP Cadre Disaster Workforce. In addition, program staff currently provides some level of support on EHP compliance issues. This varies widely between programs and HQ/regional offices. The capabilities will be further augmented with the utilization of pre-identified and trained resources from local, State, Federal, Tribal and Territorial partners. These individuals have the necessary knowledge and resources to provide EHP policy direction and technical expertise to support the timely and compliant delivery of the Agency's mission and Programs.

When complete, FEMA Programs will have integrated capabilities to consider EHP requirements early in the Programs' or projects' planning and development phases.

OBJECTIVE 1.1: STRENGTHEN EHP HUMAN CAPITAL

To adequately fulfill its EHP compliance responsibilities, FEMA requires a commitment of competent human capital workforce/technicians/employees/public servants who are knowledgeable about FEMA's missions and in particular EHP compliance issues. This workforce should include a full range of skilled human capital resources including those within OEHP, FEMA programs, and our partners. OEHP is able to engage in EHP reviews, make appropriate compliance determinations, evaluate technical EHP information, engage in interagency consultation, and make recommendations to decision-makers in a timely manner. OEHP has a synergistic relationship with FEMA's programs and partners. To better integrate the EHP requirements into FEMA's mission, OEHP provides training and technical assistance that builds capabilities within Federal, State, local, Territorial and Tribal programs and partners.

In alignment with FEMA's Strategic Goals 4 and 5, we will strengthen our human capital by attracting, retaining, and cultivating a workforce that meets the ever-changing demands placed upon FEMA staff and the EHP disaster workforce. In doing so, FEMA staff will have appropriate EHP capabilities and competencies to perform duties and workloads. The EHP workforce is a multi-disciplined team that will have expertise in all of the EHP competencies and successfully meet resource demands under varying situations, including both daily operations and during disasters or catastrophic situations. The workforce will be highly qualified and utilize proactive strategies to recruit, train, manage, and retain employees that are actively engaged in and committed to achieving FEMA's mission objectives. Employees will be trained, credentialed, and experienced in coordinating with FEMA programs to ensure efficient program compliance. In order to achieve this goal, it will need to be supported by FEMA management with staffing and financial resources.

Though this plan addresses the needs to build a baseline EHP Human Capital capability, it will be important to re-assess human capital needs based on the impacts of: 1) efficiencies gained from other elements of the Strategic Plan; 2) program changes with major business impacts; 3) significant changes in operational planning assumptions; and 3) needs resulting from shifts in required EHP competencies. This will occur as part of the regular strategic planning cycle, or as needed based on above program changes.

Strategy 1.1.1: Identify required EHP capabilities and staffing levels across FEMA necessary to achieve the mission.

Description: FEMA will develop an inventory of EHP capabilities and staffing levels needed to achieve adequate integration of EHP responsibilities across all of the Agency's programs and missions. It will also provide unbiased oversight for ensuring integrity of FEMA's EHP responsibilities.

FEMA will first take inventory of the current levels of its EHP permanent workforce, at Headquarters and in the Regions, as well as its EHP disaster workforce. FEMA will then identify gaps in areas where staffing and/or EHP expertise is not adequate, based on targeted levels required for daily operations and surge situations during disasters and catastrophic situations. The identification of key EHP responsibilities and required qualifications are essential for establishing both the current and future staffing needs. EHP's credentialing initiative will assist in establishing capability needs for the EHP disaster workforce. The outcome of this strategy will be a gap analysis of EHP capabilities and staffing levels within FEMA. The strategy will lay the foundation for all EHP human capital planning – and the resulting gap analysis will feed into the Human Capital Plan and Training Strategy of Objectives 1.1.2 and 1.1.3, respectively.

Key Participants:

Lead: OEHP

Support: Office of Chief Human Capital Officer, Program Proponents [Public Assistance, Individual Assistance, Federal Insurance and Mitigation Administration, Grant Programs Directorate, Logistics Directorate, Support Services and Facilities Management Division, and other Programs with actions that may need to comply with EHP requirements], Emergency Management Institute (EMI), Disaster Reserve Workforce Division

Implementation Steps:

Year 1: Establish working group to review and identify required EHP competencies, conduct inventory of existing competencies, and conduct a gap analysis for needed talent and resources. Complete assessment and gap analysis.

Year 2: Follow-up work from this assessment will be addressed in Strategy 1.1.2.

Strategy 1.1.2: Develop Human Capital Plan based on FEMA-wide EHP competencies.

Description: FEMA will develop a Human Capital Plan (HCP) for EHP in accordance with established requirements from the Office of Personnel Management (OPM) and FEMA. The plan will address the key areas of Human Capital: strategic alignment, talent management, leadership and knowledge management, performance management and accountability, now and in the future, in order to best fulfill EHP's mission. The plan, and in particular the section focusing on strategic alignment, will leverage the outcomes from Strategy 1.1.1.

The components of talent management include recruitment/sourcing, position fulfillment, staffing analysis, and employee retention. OEHP will work closely with the FEMA Office of the Chief Human Capital Officer to develop approaches for effective recruitment, position fulfillment, and employee retention. Strategy 1.1.1 and EHP's credentialing initiative are critical for developing the staffing analysis.

A knowledge management plan will enable the EHP workforce to perform their job functions effectively. Knowledge development will occur through classroom instruction, on-line courses, on-the-job training/diversified experience, mentoring and performance coaching. EHP's credentialing initiative will assist in identifying the knowledge gaps and targets.

OEHP will continue to use their current Performance Scorecard as a method to ensure performance management and accountability. OEHP will utilize Employee Performance Plans (aligned to the OEHP Performance Scorecards and other program performance systems) to define employees' individual goals and tasks.

Key Participants:

Lead: OEHP

Support: Office of Chief Human Capital Officer, Office of Policy and Program Analysis, Program Proponents, EMI, Disaster Reserve Workforce Division, EHP Advisory Committee (EHPAC), EHP Training Advisory Committee

Implementation Steps:

Year 1: Strategically align EHP function to HC needs.

Year 2: Upon completion of Strategy 1.1.1 and in conjunction with the working group, develop timeline and approach to HCP; Begin benchmarking practices and identifying best practices for HC.

Year 3: Complete HCP and begin implementation of findings.

Year 3-5: Continue implementation of recommendations.

Strategy 1.1.3: Develop a comprehensive EHP Education and Training Strategy.

Description: A comprehensive EHP Education and Training Strategy will build from FEMA's current existing EHP courses and identify needed revisions and delivery schedules in the upcoming five years. FEMA will build from the existing capabilities and staffing level Gap Analysis developed as a result of Strategy 1.1.1, as well as the Leadership & Knowledge Management aspects of 1.1.2. The scale and scope of this ongoing effort to improve training and knowledge processed will extend beyond the OEHP staff to include those identified with EHP competencies to include Agency officials, Program managers and staff and FEMA partners. This strategy will take into consideration changes or specialized training requirements resulting from the efforts of Objective 2.1[1].

FEMA's current EHP courses do not address all the needs of the EHP function or FEMA's programs. The Agency's credentialing initiative will identify gaps that should be addressed in the EHP courses. In addition, existing courses may not be adequately tailored for some audiences, like staff from new programs, partners and stakeholders, and may need new courses or outreach materials to account for these. The strategy will develop a framework to adequately meet the training needs of the EHP function staff, program staff, and other audiences to include FEMA partners and stakeholders.

FEMA's present EHP courses will be revised and updated to incorporate the policy, program and operational changes within the Agency that have occurred in the past three years. The Training Strategy will identify the approach to achieve the revision of all courses and additions of new courses by FY13.

OEHP and Emergency Management Institute (EMI) will develop a comprehensive schedule of course offerings to ensure the training needs as identified in this Strategy are met.

Key Participants:

Lead: OEHP, EMI

Support: EHP Training working group, Representatives from Program Proponents as needed; Disaster Reserve Workforce Division

Implementation Steps:

Year 2-3: Establish standing EHP Training working group and complete training needs assessment; Identify shortfalls, prioritize needs and develop/revise courses by priority; Pilot/delivery of courses.

Year 3-5: Continue to develop revise and deliver courses. Assess effectiveness of revised/developed courses.

---

[1] Objective 2.1: Simplify, Standardize, and Improve the EHP Compliance Process Across All Programs

Strategy 1.1.4: Strengthen EHP capabilities with State, Tribal, and Territorial partners.

Description: FEMA recognizes the need to build EHP capabilities within State, Tribal, and Territorial agencies and offices to improve the consideration of EHP requirements in applications for Federal assistance. Early identification of EHP resources or issues by these applicants and partners, as well as possible mitigation or avoidance measures, may substantially shorten the duration of FEMA's EHP compliance review process. FEMA will identify opportunities to deliver training and outreach to these applicants and partners. In addition, this strategy will identify mechanisms for increasing capability at the State/Tribal/Territorial level.

With increased capabilities, these partners will be better positioned to deliver FEMA programs effectively. This strategy works in concert with Goal 3, Strengthen Partnerships.

Key Participants:

Lead: OEHP, EMI

Support: EHPAC, State/Tribal/Territorial partners, Chief Financial Officer (CFO), Chief Procurement Officer, EHP Training working group, External Affairs, Program Proponents as needed

Implementation Steps:

Year 3: Identify potential resources among State/Tribal/Territorial partners. Work with State/Tribal/Territorial partners to review capabilities and perform gap analysis.

Year 4: Identify shortfalls and training requirements. Develop plan to deliver the training and outreach to State/Tribal/Territorial partners.

Year 4-5: Secure funding to train non-FEMA personnel; Develop or revise existing training as identified; Work with States, Tribes and Territories to deliver training.

OBJECTIVE 1.2: DEVELOP AN INVESTMENT AND FUNDING SUPPORT STRATEGY TO MEET FEMA'S EHP COMPLIANCE GOALS AND PROGRAM METRICS.

The success of FEMA's EHP function will rely on appropriate funding and strategic investments that will allow it to fulfill its mission commensurate with legislative and regulatory requirements. Additionally, new programs have been integrated into FEMA from other DHS entities, increasing the demand for strategic solutions and approaches to meet the national EHP policies and requirements.

FEMA must establish a baseline resource allocation that will achieve the most effective implementation and integration of national EHP policies into the Agency's mission and programs. This includes stable and consistent funding that supports compliance and also allows for strategic investments in integrated systems and staff. Critical components of this objective are the establishment of an EHP business case and the use of enterprise systems to measure workloads, performance, and budgets.

Strategy 1.2.1: Develop a business case justifying the need to fund EHP capabilities required to effectively meet our FEMA mission.

Description: OEHP will develop a business case that establishes the Agency's requirements to support EHP and thereby justifying a baseline resource allocation for the EHP function. This effort will tie in with the effort in Strategy 1.1.1 which identifies capability and resource needs for EHP compliance across the Agency. To date, a baseline resource allocation has never been established. The business case will also provide an investment strategy for implementing the various strategies in this Strategic Plan.

Finally, this business case will be the baseline source for the Future Year Homeland Security Program (FYHSP), over guidance requests (OGRs), unfunded requests (UFRs), and other requirements within FEMA's PPBE[2] cycle. A draft of the business case will be vetted with internal and external stakeholders resulting in a final deliverable for senior leadership decision-making.

Key Participants:

Lead: OEHP

Support: EHP Advisory Committee (EHPAC), Chief Financial Officer (CFO), Office of Policy and Program Analysis, Program Proponents

Implementation Steps:

Year 1: Develop business case and obtain funding.

Year 2-5: Update business case to align to annual operations plan and input from Human Capital analysis (from Objective 1.1).

---

[2] Planning, Programming, Budgeting, Execution

Strategy 1.2.2: Utilize integrated technologies to improve data-driven decision making capabilities.

Description: FEMA will leverage system technologies, such as enterprise systems, to enable OEHP to identify, gather and report data that provides the foundation for program management, operational and strategic decisions, and program evaluation. Strategy 1.2.2 is intricately linked to Objective 2.2 and 2.3[3] of this strategic plan. Strategy 1.2.2 will encompass the need for any identification, acquisition, and operational maintenance of the appropriate technology that supports the business case.

Key Participants:

Lead: Office of the Chief Information Officer (CIO), OEHP

Support: Program Proponents

Implementation Steps:

Year 1-5: Includes 2 deployments of Data Warehouse to support OEHP requirements per year. The Enterprise Data Warehouse (EDW) was created to make data from FEMA's various web-based systems (e.g. grants management) accessible to users across the Agency. Field staff, as well as headquarters and regional personnel, can access the Data Warehouse to perform ad-hoc reporting, on-line data analysis, evaluate trends and decide where best to assign resources to accomplish FEMA's strategic goals. Rapid, customizable access to high quality data can lead to improved efficiencies in disaster mitigation, preparedness, and response and recovery efforts.

---

[3] Objective 2.2: Leverage Technology in Compliance Process
Objective 2.3: Evaluation of Compliance Process

GOAL 2: STRENGTHEN OPERATIONAL EFFECTIVENESS

> "...wetlands prevent an estimated $23 billion in annual damage from hurricane winds and flooding in the Northeast and Gulf Coast..." ~The Day (Connecticut) ~

FEMA will strengthen the operational effectiveness of EHP compliance by implementing a standardized compendium of regulations, management directives, policies, procedures, systems and tools to support and manage EHP compliance. In addition, FEMA will use strategic investments of resources (EHP Strategic Goal 1) in national decision-making to leverage capabilities and take advantage of streamlining opportunities.

This goal supports FEMA's strategic goal of leading an integrated approach that strengthens the Nation's ability to address disasters, emergencies and acts of terrorism, as well as the goal of providing FEMA assistance in an easily accessible and coordinated manner.[4] Engaging our partners, most notably Program Proponents, will be critical in achieving this goal.

Strengthened operational effectiveness of the EHP compliance process will result in a more reliable, timely and cost effective compliance process, and more informed decision-making at all levels within FEMA.

OBJECTIVE 2.1: SIMPLIFY, STANDARDIZE AND IMPROVE THE EHP COMPLIANCE PROCESS ACROSS ALL PROGRAMS.

FEMA recognizes there are EHP compliance efficiencies that could be achieved within and across programs. These efficiencies will be achieved by integrating EHP considerations into program policies and grant requirements and procedures. In addition, streamlining can be achieved by pursuing programmatic approaches which take advantage of the uniqueness of each program, group of activities or project types, or geographic area without jeopardizing overall compliance or compromising the value that EHP adds to society.

A programmatic approach is often an effective and efficient means of meeting the intent and purpose of various EHP requirements. It enables FEMA to move beyond the minimum level of compliance required for each individual action and evaluate the impacts to the human

---

[4] FEMA Strategic Plan 2008, Goal 1

** Published on Monday, September 22, 2008 by The Day (Connecticut) - Wetlands - Nature's 'Horizontal Levees' - Blunt Storm Damage Recent study puts a dollar value on their ability to protect coast, by Judy Benson

environment in a holistic way taking into consideration various cumulative effects and complex situations.

Strategy 2.1.1: Align FEMA environmental procedures to DHS Management Directives.

Description: Through a combination of Regulations and Management Directive(s), FEMA plans to revise its environmental requirements and procedures. The new changes are expected to integrate FEMA's responsibilities under the National Environmental Policy Act (NEPA) with responsibilities under several other EHP requirements that are frequently triggered by Agency actions, including the National Historic Preservation Act (NHPA), Endangered Species Act, Clean Water Act, Executive Order 12898 – Environmental Justice, and others. The revised procedures are expected to align historic FEMA and DHS regulations and policies, while also addressing FEMA's unique missions and authorities including grant-related, disaster-related, and emergency authorities. FEMA expects that the new procedures will take into account FEMA's many organizational and programmatic changes and support the new FEMA vision.

The new procedures are intended to standardize the EHP review process by establishing the minimum level of review and compliance required for all FEMA actions, including approval of projects or programs and the issuance of regulations, policies, procedures, and grant guidance.

In addition, FEMA hopes to integrate EHP requirements and needs into the development and implementation of Environmental Management Systems (EMSs) throughout the Agency, an effort led by FEMA's Occupational Safety, Health and Environment Division.

Key Participants:

Lead: OEHP

Support: DHS Office of Occupational Safety and Environmental Programs (OSEP), DHS Office of General Counsel, FEMA Program Proponents, FEMA's Occupational Safety, Health and Environment Division (OSHE, lead for EMS), Office of Policy and Program Analysis, Office of Chief Counsel, and other Federal agencies who set policy or oversee the management of particular natural or biological resources or historic properties (CEQ, ACHP, FWS, NMFS, etc.).

Implementation Steps:

Step 1: Draft Notice of Proposed Rulemaking and Draft FEMA Management Directive

Step 2: Provide for Public Comment

Step 3: Draft Final Rulemaking and Final FEMA Management Directive

Strategy 2.1.2: Develop and implement an EHP policy framework.

Description: FEMA staff will develop and implement policies, Agency-wide where applicable, on EHP compliance. The purpose of these EHP policies is to ensure consistency across programs, facilitate compliance with the multiple EHP requirements, and to ensure that the intent and purpose of EHP requirements are effectively integrated and satisfied within the Agency. OEHP and Program Proponents will collaborate in the development of this framework to ensure the right EHP policy issues are identified and prioritized. Utilizing the framework, FEMA will evaluate the applicability and effectiveness of the policies on a recurring basis to update, revise, or remove as appropriate.

Key Participants:

Lead: OEHP

Support: Program Proponents, Office of Policy and Program Analysis, Office of Chief Counsel, Policy Working Group (PWG), EHP Advisory Committee (EHPAC)

Implementation Steps:

Year 1: Establish standing EHP Policy Working Group (PWG); develop and finalize policy framework and fit existing policies into that framework.

Year 2-5: Revise and develop policies based on priority list (2 per year)

Strategy 2.1.3: Create and disseminate FEMA-wide EHP guidance documents.

Description: OEHP will develop/update EHP guidance documents to effectively implement the new EHP Regulations and MDs (see 2.1.1) and EHP policies (see 2.1.2). Guidance documents provide the appropriate level of detail needed to ensure that new Regs/MDs and policies are implemented and integrated effectively, seamlessly, and consistently into the Agency's mission, Programs and operations. Strategy 2.1.3 links to EHP Strategic Goal 3.

EHP guidance documents and standard operating procedures will be made available through an on-line library and readily available to Agency staff or partners.

Key Participants:

Lead: OEHP

Support: Program Proponents, Office of Chief Counsel, OSHE Division, Office of Policy and Program Analysis

Implementation Steps:

Prioritize, develop, and refine guidance documents on a yearly basis.

Strategy 2.1.4: Develop a strategy to improve and standardize FEMA's compliance with Executive Order 11988 (Floodplain Management) and Executive Order 11990 (Wetlands Protection).

Description: As the Nation's preeminent emergency management and preparedness Agency, the Federal Insurance Administrator of the National Flood Insurance Program and Fund, and the leading technical expert for implementation of Executive Order (EO) 11988 (Floodplain Management), FEMA must lead the Federal Government by example in its compliance with EO 11988 as well as EO 11990 (Wetlands Protection).

FEMA will re-energize its efforts to set a Federal Government standard for implementation of EO 11988 and EO 11990. In addition, FEMA will develop a strategy to address the Agency's internal coordination and compliance efforts regarding the implementing procedures codified in 44 CFR Part 9. The strategy will address the following areas: Agency policies for addressing compliance with 44 CFR 9, capabilities needed to ensure adequate review of the Agency's actions under 44 CFR 9, and training and outreach for program staff and partners.

Key Participants:

Lead: OEHP

Support: Program Proponents, Office of Policy and Program Analysis, Office of Chief Counsel, stakeholders/partners (e.g. The Association of State Floodplain Managers (ASFPM)).

Implementation Steps:

Year 1: Establish Working Group to guide strategy development. Draft implementation strategy.

Years 2: Vet and finalize strategy.

Years 3-5: Implementation of strategy.

Strategy 2.1.5: Develop nation-wide approaches for compliance with Section 106 of the National Historic Preservation Act.

Description: OEHP will work with the President's Advisory Council on Historic Preservation (ACHP), the National Conference of State Historic Preservation Officers (NCSHPO), and Tribal governments and organizations to develop Nation-wide approaches for review of Agency actions under Section 106 of the National Historic Preservation Act. This is a critical effort toward standardizing and streamlining the Section 106 review process and consultation and documentation requirements for typical Agency actions and grant-funded projects. In many cases it will eliminate the need for Section 106 consultation on individual projects. (Per 36 CFR 800.14)

Key Participants:

Lead: OEHP

Support: Program Proponents, Office of Chief Counsel, ACHP, NCSHPO, National Association of Tribal Historic Preservation Officers (NATHPO)

Implementation Steps:

Year 1: Define and request resource requirements to complete this strategy.

Year 2: Begin development of Nation-wide approaches and initiate consultation efforts.

Year 3: Continue consultation and development of Nation-wide approaches.

Year 4: Finalize and implement Nation-wide approaches.

Strategy 2.1.6: Develop Regional & State programmatic approaches to further streamline EHP review.

Description: FEMA can achieve efficiencies in its EHP compliance process by developing geographic-based programmatic approaches. Examples of these geographic programmatic approaches include the development of Statewide Programmatic Agreements for NHPA Section 106 compliance, Statewide Programmatic Environmental Assessments for a particular group or groups of actions, Memoranda of Understanding or Memoranda of Agreement with State Resource Agencies, and regional analyses or protocols with particular stakeholders.

Based on past experience, OEHP will identify when opportunities exist to pursue geographic-based programmatic approaches. Program Proponents will assist in the prioritization and development of these initiatives to ensure adequate commitment to these approaches.

Key Participants:

Lead: OEHP

Support: Office of Chief Counsel

Implementation Steps:

Years 1-5: Prioritize, develop and implement programmatic approaches on a yearly basis.

OBJECTIVE 2.2: INTEGRATE EHP REQUIREMENTS INTO PROGRAM GOALS, DEVELOPMENT, IMPLEMENTATION AND PERFORMANCE.

In order to achieve operational effectiveness for EHP compliance across FEMA, each program must integrate the EHP requirements and FEMA-wide compliance approaches into all aspects of program operation and implementation. This includes identifying ways that each program can utilize the EHP requirements to best inform program decision-making at the policy and project level, and then integrating these requirements into the formulation of policy, program guidance, training, systems and documentation, as well as building EHP technical capabilities to support program needs. In working with OEHP and FEMA-wide EHP performance metrics, program offices will also set and track performance metrics for EHP compliance, and regularly evaluate their programs' EHP compliance based on FEMA-wide standards in order to identify ways to improve the overall effectiveness of the EHP compliance process.

Strategy 2.2.1: Review current program policies and implementation procedures to identify areas where new authorities, program changes or existing procedures can better integrate EHP requirements and values, consistent with the FEMA and program mission.

Description: Program policies, changes and new authorities often impact the implementation of EHP requirements within a particular FEMA program. Program Proponents, with technical guidance from OEHP, will examine current procedures to integrate EHP requirements, and identify whether changes need to be made to address requirements that are not currently met, revise program processes to integrate EHP into national level program implementation and decision-making, and identify whether adequate resources are budgeted to meet EHP compliance needs. In addition, Program Proponents will evaluate whether there are other ways to modify program implementation to better incorporate and address EHP values, especially those consistent and supportive of the FEMA and program mission (such as those that protect floodplains, wetlands, coastal barriers, habitat, or historic/cultural elements important for communities to protect from natural or man-made incidents or acts of terrorism).

Key Participants:

Lead: Program Proponents

Support: OEHP, Policy Working Group (PWG)

Implementation Steps:

Year 2: Initial program assessment.

Year 3-5: Make regular adjustments as necessary and in conjunction with the results from evaluations under Strategy 2.4.2.

Strategy 2.2.2: Develop and monitor program specific EHP metrics to measure progress in the integration of EHP requirements.

Description: In order to track and measure the changes made to program procedures and processes as a result of Strategy 2.3.1 and 2.4.2, it will be important for each Program Proponent to develop program-specific metrics to track and measure progress in the integration of EHP requirements.

Key Participants:

Lead: Program Proponents

Support: OEHP

Implementation Steps:

Year 2: Initial development of program EHP metrics.

Year 3-5: Make regular adjustments as necessary and in conjunction with the results from evaluations under Strategy 2.4.2.

OBJECTIVE 2.3: LEVERAGE TECHNOLOGY IN THE EHP COMPLIANCE PROCESS.

FEMA will standardize the use of the existing EHP Management Information System (EMIS) to: manage and document EHP compliance for all FEMA mission programs and activities; enhance its development to ensure ease of use for grant applicants and other customers both internal and external to FEMA; maximize automation capabilities; and create seamless interfaces with program systems.

FEMA will also integrate technological capabilities, such as Geographic Information Systems (GIS), and the development of new technologies in the EHP compliance process. Leveraging available technologies and standardized support systems is one of the most critical efforts to achieve strengthened operational effectiveness, through improved reliability, timeliness and cost effectiveness of the EHP compliance process.

Strategy 2.3.1: Institutionalize the Environmental Planning and Historic Preservation Management System (EMIS) as part of a FEMA Enterprise System.

Description: FEMA will justify the use of EMIS as an Enterprise System across FEMA to standardize the electronic data collection and storage and decision-making for the EHP compliance review of Agency actions. This justification should include a complete package documenting the system purpose and need, future development including external capabilities, and prioritized plans for interface/integration with current or new systems. OEHP and Program

Proponents shall coordinate during requirements gathering and system development efforts to ensure there is an appropriate interface between EMIS and DHS Grants Management system of choice and any other management system that FEMA may seek to develop in the future.

Key Participants:

Lead: OEHP, Chief Information Officer (CIO)

Support: Program Proponents, Office of Management and Budget (OMB), Records Management, Office of Policy and Program Analysis, Grants Management Systems Steering Group and Program Management Office

Implementation Steps:

Year 1: Establish EMIS standing working group to guide EMIS development; Develop justification and development package for EMIS; Develop requirements for interface between EMIS and DHS Grants Management systems (and others as appropriate).

Year 2: Deploy EMIS interface; Develop requirements for external EMIS; Gain OMB approval for external EMIS.

Year 3: Develop and test external EMIS; Deploy external EMIS.

Years 1-5: Deploy EMIS internal system enhancements (1 per quarter).

Years 2-5: Secure annual budgeting for EMIS maintenance and enhancement/development.

Strategy 2.3.2: Develop approaches to integrate GIS and other technologies into the EHP compliance process.

Description: EHP requirements typically address geographically-identifiable resources such as floodplains, historic properties, coastal areas, rivers and streams, habitat, etc. The use of Geographic Information Systems (GIS) and other resource identification and management technologies (e.g. Fish and Wildlife Service's IPAC system) for both FEMA's planning efforts and individual program and project implementation significantly improves the ability to identify natural or biological resources or historic properties that may be present in a given area. Use of GIS reduces the duration of FEMA's EHP review, and also provides the ability to identify and evaluate cumulative effects of actions taken by the Agency or other proponents, thereby providing a holistic and more accurate picture of impacts on EHP resources.

OEHP will coordinate internally with the FEMA GIS Working Group and continue to coordinate closely with the National Park Service (NPS) to implement national GIS data standards for historic properties damaged by disasters. FEMA will also explore opportunities to partner with other Federal Agencies that have GIS expertise to further the goals of FEMA's mission and meet the intent of the various EHP requirements through GIS-related initiatives.

Key Participants:

Lead: OEHP, CIO

Support: Program Proponents, Other Federal Agencies (NPS, USFWS)

Implementation Steps:

Year 2: Conduct technology needs assessment and conduct outreach to CIO, Program proponents, other Federal agencies, etc. to identify and assess existing technological capabilities.

Year 3: Draft strategies and determine resource needs.

Year 4: Obtain approval of senior leadership.

Year 5: Pilot test systems/technology approaches; System implementation.

OBJECTIVE 2.4: EVALUATE THE RELIABILITY, CONSISTENCY, COST-EFFECTIVENESS, AND TIMELINESS OF FEMA'S EHP COMPLIANCE.

Evaluating FEMA's EHP performance is essential to identifying the Agency's progress in achieving its EHP Strategic Goals and ensuring that the compliance process is reliable, cost-effective and timely. Measuring performance in these areas will ensure a holistic and accurate evaluation of FEMA's EHP compliance efforts, and provide indicators for areas that may need greater resources. In addition, an evaluation approach will be developed along various places in the compliance lifecycle, providing short-term, intermediate, and long-term forecasts of progress and expected outcomes.

Strategy 2.4.1: Establish performance management system for EHP.

Description: FEMA has an established set of FEMA-wide EHP performance metrics, which are based on FEMA program performance goals and EHP strategic objectives. Building upon the established metrics, OEHP will work with the EHP Advisory Committee and Regional offices to validate and mature program-level and region-specific metrics and targets each year, and establish a performance management system for review and validation on a quarterly basis, program and regional input for revisions, and EHP/program changes or resource needs to improve performance.

This effort will require Enterprise Data Warehouse and EMIS capabilities to collect and report on data in support of FEMA-wide EHP performance management goals.

These metrics will also support various aspects of the EHP Strategic Plan including development of the business case, identification of resource and capability gaps, and identification of the effectiveness of programmatic solutions to EHP compliance.

Key Participants:

Lead: OEHP

Support: EHPAC, Program Proponents, Office of Policy and Program Analysis

Implementation Steps:

Year 1: Establish performance metrics based on data from baseline year (FY08); refine performance management process based on regional and EHP Advisory Committee feedback; develop/refine Data Warehouse and EMIS capabilities to support new performance metric data; develop quality metrics based on program evaluation methodology.

Year 2: Integrate key metrics into Future Year Homeland Security Program (FYHSP).

Years 3-5: Continue to evaluate the effectiveness of metrics in documenting EHP performance and revise as needed.

Strategy 2.4.2: Conduct Program-level analyses and provide recommendations for improving the integration of EHP requirements into FEMA Programs.

Description: FEMA will identify opportunities where program-level EHP analyses would improve the efficiency of the EHP compliance process, particularly through time and costs savings. The assessment or evaluation of individual Programs may reveal areas of significant concern in a Program that trigger EHP requirements, and thereby allow FEMA to focus resources in those particular areas.

The EHP Advisory Committee (see Strategy 3.1.3) will develop a standardized methodology for conducting EHP analyses for FEMA Programs. This methodology will utilize a consistent process and criteria to evaluate Program maturity in integrating EHP requirements, based on both qualitative and quantitative data and will tie into FEMA's EHP performance metrics. This methodology will address the frequency of the evaluations and resources required to conduct the evaluations.

The analyses will provide critical performance information to Program managers and Senior Leadership to inform decision-making on programmatic process changes, policy changes, and resource needs.

Key Participants:

Lead: OEHP

Support: EHPAC, Program Proponents, Office of Policy and Program Analysis, OHSE

Implementation Steps:

Year 1: Complete on-going Program evaluations (e.g. Unified Hazard Mitigation Assistance, GPD Programmatic Environmental Assessment).

Year 2: Validate methodology and develop evaluation approach and timeline; secure needed resources.

Year 3: Begin to evaluate programs based on timeline.

Year 4: Expand to programs in other Directorates.

GOAL 3: STRENGTHEN PARTNERSHIPS

As the coordinator of Federal disaster/incident preparedness, protection, response, recovery and mitigation, FEMA relies on strong partnerships to ensure success in carrying out its mission. Many different partners and stakeholders have specific roles and responsibilities in meeting FEMA's environmental planning and historic preservation (EHP) requirements. This shared responsibility makes strong coordination essential throughout FEMA's program implementation and EHP compliance process to ensure mission success.

Coordination is essential among OEHP, all FEMA program offices, other DHS components and counterparts such as Occupational Safety and Environmental Programs (OSEP) and other Federal agencies with emergency management, resource management/protection, or EHP compliance roles. FEMA must also work closely with partners external to FEMA such as tribal governments, states, territories, local governments, regional and state resource agencies, EHP interest groups and organizations, and the public.

Among these key partners are those impacted by disasters and/or those receiving FEMA grant assistance, stakeholders with an interest in the assistance that FEMA is providing to communities, and resource agencies who work with OEHP to ensure FEMA meets its legal requirements under the various Environmental and Historic Preservation laws, Executive Orders, and regulations.

Strengthened partnerships will result in increased awareness in support of the EHP function and the value of EHP, a better utilization of resources across FEMA, adoption of best practices and creative compliance solutions, more effective and transparent FEMA decision-making and program delivery, better use of opportunities to create linkages with preparedness and planning activities to reduce the overall impact of disasters on the human environment, and ultimately improved EHP compliance.

OBJECTIVE 3.1: INCREASE AWARENESS OF THE VALUE OF THE EHP COMPLIANCE PROCESS ACROSS FEMA PROGRAMS AND AMONG STAKEHOLDERS, IN ORDER TO FOSTER A SENSE OF OWNERSHIP OF AND RESPONSIBILITY FOR EHP COMPLIANCE.

In order to achieve an improved balance between shared EHP responsibilities and ultimately a more effective EHP compliance process, OEHP will coordinate with FEMA programs and partners to increase awareness of EHP requirements, processes, and responsibilities, as well as to highlight the value that the EHP compliance process can add to FEMA's mission and program implementation.

When Objective 3.1 is achieved, FEMA will actively promote EHP values, benefits, and needs so that EHP compliance is understood by all FEMA stakeholders. Both internal and external partners are involved in strategic implementation of EHP requirements throughout FEMA and will actively seek to utilize the EHP compliance process to enhance programs and activities and make informed decisions. OEHP, Program Proponents and other partners regularly will engage each other on routine program matters.

Strategy 3.1.1: Develop and implement an EHP outreach strategy.

FEMA Program Proponents and OEHP will work together to develop an outreach strategy to provide reliable and appropriate information to FEMA EHP partners and stakeholders regarding the Agency's EHP compliance requirements and process, roles and responsibilities, the value the EHP process adds to program implementation, risk awareness and communication and other key messages. Under this outreach strategy, target audiences will be identified, messages will be tailored to specific audiences as needed, and comprehensive delivery mechanisms and strategies will be deployed (e.g. use of the internet, convening national and regional EHP summits). Audiences will be prioritized with regard to their ability to advance the FEMA EHP Strategic Plan.

This strategy includes clearly defining and communicating the roles and responsibilities/expectations of the partners in the EHP compliance process, and establishing formal and informal mechanisms between Program proponents to facilitate regular communication and interaction.

Strategy 3.1.1 also includes an evaluation of existing outreach practices, methods and capabilities, identifying what is effective and available for reuse, and developing a suite of outreach materials such as guidance, brochures, fact sheets, best practices, briefings and talking points to be used by FEMA Program and OEHP staff. This Strategy links to 3.2.2.

Key Participants:

Lead: OEHP

Support: Office of the Administrator, Deputy Associate Administrator for Regional Operations, Regional Administrators, Program Proponents, Federal Coordinating Officers, Communications Section, External Affairs, Office of Chief Counsel, Tribal and State Partners, EHP Resource Agencies

Implementation Steps:

Year 1: Create EHP Outreach working group, secure contract funding; evaluate current outreach processes and gaps; develop the EHP outreach strategy; begin to develop high priority EHP outreach products.

Year 2: Fully develop suite of EHP outreach products and mechanisms for delivery.

Year 3: Deploy and utilize full suite of EHP outreach products across FEMA.

Year 4: Evaluate EHP outreach strategy and revise/update as needed.

Year 5: Implement changes to outreach strategy.

Strategy 3.1.2: Establish an EHP Advisory Committee (EHPAC) at the national level to guide the implementation of the EHP Strategic Plan.

Each FEMA Program has a variety of process requirements that lead to potential inconsistency in the implementation of EHP requirements as defined in Regulation and procedures as well as confusion among FEMA's partners and stakeholders. In addition, each program has a different level of maturity in the integration of EHP requirements and processes.

Establishing an EHPAC at the national level will serve to provide senior-level program management participation and direction in the implementation of the EHP strategic objectives across FEMA and will broaden the reach of understanding of the EHP compliance process, encourage the sharing of best practices, and enhance EHP's ability to support the FEMA mission.

Key Participants:

Lead: OEHP

Support: Deputy Associate Administrator for Regional Operations, Office of Policy and Program Analysis, Program Managers, Regional Environmental Officer (REO), Office of Chief Counsel, Disaster Reserve Workforce Division, Office of Occupational Safety and Environmental Management, Emergency Management Institute (EMI), Chief Information Officer (CIO), United States Fire Administration (USFA)

Implementation Steps:

Year 1: Establish committee and charter and conduct EHPAC kickoff meetings.

Years 2-5: Maintain according to EHPAC Charter.

OBJECTIVE 3.2: IMPROVE COORDINATION WITH RESOURCE AGENCIES.

Statutory and regulatory EHP requirements mandate FEMA to work with a wide variety of Federal and State resource agencies responsible for the management or protection of natural and biological resources and historic properties. These include organizations such as the Advisory Council on Historic Preservation (ACHP), the Council on Environmental Quality (CEQ), the Department of Interior (DOI) (e.g. National Park Service, US Fish and Wildlife Service), the United States Army Corps of Engineers (USACE), Tribal/State Historic Preservation Officers THPO/SHPO), state environmental protection and environmental quality agencies, and many others. Successful relationships and partnerships with these agencies are critical to achieve the following:

- ❖ The effective delivery of both FEMA disaster and non-disaster assistance;
- ❖ Full confidence on the part of resource agencies and stakeholders in FEMA's ability and intent to comply with EHP requirements in order to optimize compliance solutions;
- ❖ Assisting other Federal, State, Tribal, local and Territorial agencies in implementing their resource protection programs in times of disaster; and
- ❖ Minimizing risks to FEMA for legal challenge.

At present, these relationships are stronger with some resource agencies than with others, inconsistent from region to region, and do not allow for proactive engagement in regional exercises and planning activities. This leads to delays or inefficiencies in the support resource agencies provide to FEMA during disasters or on projects having complex EHP issues.

By increasing FEMA's commitment to and coordination with resource agencies, we will achieve the following:

❖ Resource agencies will be more proactively engaged in and committed to FEMA's mission;

❖ The relationships between FEMA and resource agencies will be pre-established and mutually supportive of each other; and

❖ Resource agencies will provide FEMA with ready access to their capabilities through their own authorities as well as what they can provide FEMA. Resource agencies will use FEMA as a model for creative and successful EHP compliance, and for technical assistance related to resource protection planning for disasters.

Strategy 3.2.1: Establish National & Regional Partnership Frameworks with Resource Agencies

FEMA Headquarters and regional offices each have varying strategies to engage resource agencies in the Agency's mission activities. Due to workload and staffing constraints, many of these ad hoc relationships are only in place during times of necessity (i.e. during disasters or project-specific consultations).

This strategy will establish a partnership framework through memorandums of understanding or similar agreements to outline how FEMA would engage with specific resource agencies on a broad level. Further, FEMA will coordinate with resources agencies to identify their compliance requirements, initiatives and best practices and incorporate them into program implementation. This framework will allow regional counterparts to in turn tier agreements based on regional needs.

Strategy 3.2.1 will result in more consistent planning and communication with resource agencies regarding mutual expectations, coordination, and roles and needs in non-disaster and disaster operations.

Key Participants:

Lead: OEHP

Support: EHP Resource Agencies, EHPAC, Office of Chief Counsel

Implementation Steps:

Year 2: Prioritize needs (Agencies).

Year 3: Initiate Pilot.

Year 4: Implement.

Year 5: Put agreements in place with "Top 3" prioritized agencies.

Strategy 3.2.2: Utilize National & Regional forums and exercises to engage resource agencies in FEMA activities.

This strategy will incorporate EHP issues and resource Agency partners, including Emergency Support Function (ESF) 11 (natural, cultural and historic resources component) into existing national and regional coordination meetings, forums, and exercises to increase awareness and opportunities for building relationships in a non-disaster and more routine setting. Specific opportunities include:

- ❖ Regional Interagency Steering Committee Meetings (RISC)
- ❖ Regional Advisory Council (RAC) Quarterly Meetings
- ❖ National and Regional Exercises
- ❖ National Emergency Management Association (NEMA) Meetings

Key Participants:

Lead: OEHP

Support: HQ Program Proponents Senior Leadership, Regional Administrators and Regional Federal Insurance and Mitigation Administration, Regional External Affairs Directors, Relevant ESFs, Resource Agencies

Implementation Steps:

Year 2: Identify and prioritize forums and exercises that would benefit from resource Agency participation and engagement; HQ and each region include resource agencies in at least one of these opportunities in the next 12 months.

Years 3-5: OEHP will work with Program Proponents, ESFs and resource agencies to implement as staff resources can support.

Strategy 3.2.3: Advocate FEMA's EHP best practices to resource agencies at the national and regional levels.

In order to continue to optimize the use of creative EHP compliance strategies to meet FEMA's unique mission requirements, it is critical to have the support and feedback from resource agencies. Although these strategies and approaches have been implemented in specific states or regions, their value is not fully understood or recognized internally to FEMA or nationally among resource agencies. The focus in this strategy is to document and share EHP's successes with resource agencies at the national, regional and state levels, and ultimately adopt these best practices nationally.

This strategy is closely linked to 3.1.1 as outreach materials may include best practices or other information targeted to resource agencies.

Key Participants:

Lead: OEHP

Support: Federal Coordinating Officers, External Affairs, Regional Administrators, Communication/Outreach

Implementation Steps:

Year 1: Utilize resources in regional offices and Joint Field Offices (JFOs) to identify and develop success stories/creative strategies to share within FEMA and with the resource agencies.

Year 2: Create mechanisms to share best practices that can be utilized by FEMA and resource agencies.

Year 3: Continue create mechanisms to share best practices and update as needed.

> **"...80% of collecting [cultural] institutions do not have an emergency or disaster plan that includes collections, with staff trained to carry it out. Because of this, more than 2.6 billion items are at risk..."**
>
> **~The Heritage Health Index Report~**

OBJECTIVE 3.3: DEVELOP AND IMPLEMENT EHP PARTNERING OPPORTUNITIES TO ADVANCE THE FEMA MISSION.

One of FEMA's goals is to lead an integrated approach[5] that strengthens the Nation's ability to address disasters, emergencies and acts of terrorism. The EHP function supports the objectives under this goal by providing proactive and creative technical assistance to strategically integrate environmental stewardship, sustainability and historic preservation into these emergency management activities in order to capitalize on complementary policy goals. Protection and stewardship of natural resources including floodplains, wetlands, coastal barriers, forests, and other natural landscapes provides increased protection to communities from natural hazards. Cultural and historic resources, such as historic buildings and districts, museum collections, and family photographs, provide disaster victims with important connections to their families and communities and a sense of place that are critical in the recovery and re-building process.

This strategic integration can occur by engaging EHP stakeholders in mission-related preparedness, planning, risk identification and reduction measures, and long term community recovery to ensure that emergency management priorities are balanced with broader community, state, tribal, territorial and national policies and values which may be related to environmental

---

[5] FEMA 2008 Strategic Plan, Goal 1

stewardship, sustainability and cultural heritage (and possibly economic values such as heritage tourism).

Full utilization of EHP partnering opportunities at the State, Tribal, local, Territorial and national level will result in more sustainable and safer communities, and ensuring that EHP value is taken into account in program decisions and project development for FEMA assistance.

Strategy 3.3.1: Incorporate EHP considerations into protection, planning, mitigation and preparedness elements of FEMA Programs (Link to FEMA Strategic Plan Objective 1.5).

Planning, mitigation, and preparedness activities are the foundation for community, State, Tribal and Territorial-level efforts to effectively address all-hazard events and enhance emergency management capabilities. Planning is also an opportunity to coordinate and integrate plans and programs with complementary goals, as well as an opportunity to work with various public and private stakeholders. Better integration of EHP considerations into these efforts will provide an opportunity to better link natural and cultural resource protection and environmental stewardship to community response, recovery, and risk reduction activities, balance emergency management planning interests with broader stakeholders, and ensure more successful and expedient program decisions and project development and approval. This links to Strategy 3.1.1.

Key Participants:

Lead: OEHP & FEMA Directorates/Offices with key roles in planning/preparedness requirement implementation

Support: Local communities, States, Tribes, Federal agencies and others who engage in planning activities, Resource agencies and EHP stakeholders

Implementation Steps:

Year 1: Initial OEHP/Program coordination; Develop pilot initiatives.

Year 2: Development of a FEMA-wide matrix of planning/preparedness initiatives and requirements; Identification and prioritization of EHP integration opportunities.

Years 3-5: Implementation.

Strategy 3.3.2: In partnership with the Heritage Emergency National Task Force, convene a National Forum to develop strategies to further the protection of cultural resources before, during, and after disasters.

In 1994, FEMA, Heritage Preservation, and the Getty Conservation Institute (GCI) convened a national summit to bring attention to the disaster planning issues and needs unique to cultural institutions and historic properties. The Heritage Emergency National Task Force, a group of over 40 Federal agencies and national service organizations created to protect cultural heritage from the damaging effects of natural disasters and other emergencies, was formed as an outgrowth of this summit and has been instrumental in engaging the emergency management and cultural resources communities in ways to better protect important cultural and historic resources before, during, and after disasters.

In continued partnership with Heritage Preservation and the Task Force, FEMA will examine the partnership's achievements and shortcomings over the past 14 years in order to re-energize this effort, determine how to better engage FEMA program proponents and other new partners, and identify strategies and key initiatives to continue this partnership and focus. This is even more critical because of the inclusion of the Task Force as a partner in ESF-11, the Natural, Cultural and Historic Properties component, led by the Department of the Interior (DOI).

Key Participants:

Lead: OEHP

Support: Program Proponents, Heritage Preservation, Heritage Emergency National Task Force, DOI

Implementation Steps:

Year 1: Work with Heritage Preservation, the Task Force and other partners, to develop a plan for development and implementation of a National Forum.

Year 2: Plan and implement a National Forum.

Year 3: Evaluate success and prioritize outcomes for further implementation.

Years 4-5: Begin implementing strategies as outcomes of the Forum.

Strategy 3.3.3: Support FEMA's coordination role under the National Response Framework (NRF) to coordinate consistent implementation of EHP requirements and ensure EHP stakeholders regularly participate in these efforts.

Various resource agencies under the National Response Framework (NRF) also have an interface with OEHP in a disaster, such as Emergency Support Functions (ESF) 3, 6, 10, 11 and 14, and there is a need to improve coordination with the relevant functions and agencies on EHP issues.

For example, ESF 11 (Natural, Cultural and Historic Resources component, led by the Department of Interior) is defined under the NRF but has not been fully developed. FEMA must work with the ESF partners to engage them in ways to leverage their own authorities and capabilities to support the disaster mission.

This strategy will develop a clear understanding of our role in coordinating with the various ESFs, and how ESF partner resources would be applied to provide EHP technical and direct assistance in a disaster operation, and develop an on-going forum for coordination. This strategy links to strategy 3.1.1 Outreach strategy, national/regional EHP summits and link to strategy 3.2.2 national/regional forums.

Key Participants:

Lead: NRF lead agencies with ESF-11 and 14, and EHP resource agencies as co-leads

Support: National Integration Center (NIC), Recovery Directorate, Operational Planning, and OEHP

Implementation Steps:

Year 1: Coordinate with NIC and existing Steering Committees to better understand existing mechanisms for coordination; Define OEHP roles.

Year 2-3: Convene a meeting of relevant partners to discuss strategies to improve EHP integration into the NRF.

Years 4-5: Implementation based on prioritized strategies.

Appendix A: Glossary of Terms

Capability: The ability to accomplish a mission or function resulting from the performance of one or more critical tasks under specified conditions. A capability may be delivered with any combination of properly planned, organized, equipped, trained, and exercised personnel that achieves the desired outcome. (Source: National Preparedness Guidelines, September 2007)

DHS Occupational Safety and Environmental Programs (OSEP): An organization within the DHS Office of the Chief Administrative Officer that provides the business framework for accomplishing work in four functional areas key to supporting the DHS mission: Safety and Occupational Health, Environmental Management, Energy Management, and Environmental Planning and Historic Preservation. OSEP's mission is to support and enhance DHS mission readiness by ensuring that safety, energy, and environmental programs, as established by laws, public policies, and best practices are appropriately integrated throughout activities, operations, and programs of DHS and its stakeholders.

Environment: The natural and physical environment and the relationship of people with that environment. (Source: Council on Environmental Quality's NEPA regulations at 40 CFR Part 1508)

Environmental Planning Process: The effort required to systematically address the environmental stewardship requirements put forth in public policy and law during program and project planning, development, and design, and prior to execution. This process may consist wholly or in part of an environmental impact evaluation. The environmental planning process may extend into execution, deployment, or operational phases when the need to control potential for adverse environmental impacts requires mitigation and monitoring. (DHS Directive 023-01)

Environmental Planning Program Manager (EPPM): The EPPM is required by DHS Management Directive 023-01 (Environmental Planning) and designated by the FEMA Administrator. The EPPM has the authority and responsibility for establishing and directing FEMA's Environmental Planning and Historic Preservation (EHP) Program and facilitating the functional integration of EHP requirements into FEMA mission, programs, and activities.

EHP Function: The responsibility of FEMA to ensure its actions comply with applicable environmental planning and historic preservation (EHP) laws, regulations, executive orders, and other requirements. This function includes all Directorates/offices and personnel throughout FEMA who have roles and responsibilities that support EHP compliance, including the FEMA Administrator, Office of Chief Counsel, OEHP and Program Proponents.

EHP Review: The process during which a FEMA proposed action is reviewed for compliance with appropriate environmental planning and historic preservation laws, executive orders and regulations. During this review, FEMA is required to consider the potential environmental consequences of its actions, document that analysis, and make that information available to the public for review and comment prior to carrying out the action.

Environmental Management Program (EMP): The Environmental Management Program (EMP) provides an integrated and systematic approach to managing Agency environmental activities in a manner that complies with pollution control and other applicable requirements, prevents pollution, mitigates environmental impacts and incorporates sustainable practices. The FEMA EMP encompasses various aspects of environmental management including environmental management systems, environmental compliance, pollution control and prevention, sustainable practices, environmental restoration and environmental liabilities management and planning.

FEMA Regional Offices: FEMA has ten (10) regional offices, each headed by a Regional Administrator. The Regional field structures are FEMA's permanent presence for communities and states across America. (Source: National Response Framework Resource Center Glossary of Terms)

Guidance documents: Documents that provide specific procedures or outline standardized processes for how to comply with a law, regulation, executive order, policy, or other requirement. Examples may include Standard Operating Procedures, instruction manuals, and job aids.

Historic Preservation: For FEMA purposes, this definition refers to requirements of Sections 106 and 110 of the National Historic Preservation Act (NHPA). Under NHPA, FEMA is required to consider the effects of its undertakings on historic properties. Undertakings include actions at FEMA facilities and projects funded under the agency's various grant programs. Historic property is defined as any district, building, structure, site, or object that is listed on or eligible for listing on the National Register of Historic Places because of its significance at the national, state, or local level in American history, architecture, archeology, engineering, or culture. By complying with NHPA, FEMA helps to promote the identification, preservation, enhancement and productive use of the nation's historic resources.

Human Capital: A framework of personnel policies, strategies, and practices to achieve a shared vision integrated with the Agency's Strategic Plan, which includes the following five elements: Strategic Alignment (Planning and Goal Setting), Leadership and Knowledge Management (Implementation), Results Oriented Performance Culture (Implementation), Talent Management (Implementation), Accountability (Evaluating Results). (Source: OPM Human Capital Plan)

Joint Field Office (JFO): JFO is a temporary Federal multi-agency coordination center established locally to facilitate field-level domestic incident management activity related to prevention, preparedness, response, and recovery when activated by the Secretary. The JFO provides a central location for coordination of Federal, State, local, Territorial, Tribal, non-governmental and private sector organizations with primary responsibility for activities associated with response and incident support. (Source: JFO Activation and Operations Interagency Integrated Standard Operating Procedures)

Office of Environmental and Historic Preservation (OEHP): OEHP provides support and policy direction to programs agency-wide for ensuring compliance with all applicable EHP laws, regulations, executive orders, and other requirements. The office is lead by Environmental Planning Program Manager. OEHP personnel include: 1) a permanent workforce comprised of Headquarters OEHP staff (OEHP Director, Agency Federal Preservation Officer, Agency Environmental Officer, and Support staff) and Regional OEHP staff (ten Regional Environmental Officers (REOs) and their support staff), and 2) the EHP cadre, who are reservists with EHP expertise that are utilized at Joint Field Offices during disaster operations.

Partners: Persons or organizations involved in the same mission and sharing in its risks and successes. Each is an agent for the other and is generally liable for the others' successes and failures.

Performance management: Applying the integrated processes of aligning, setting, and communicating performance expectations, monitoring performance and providing feedback, developing performance and addressing poor performance, and rating and rewarding performance in support of the organization's goals and objectives. (Source: DRAFT FEMA Performance Management, Management Directive)

Planning, Programming, Budgeting, Execution (PPBE): A four-phased process to determine program priorities and allocate resources. (Source: Department of Homeland security Management Directives System MD Number: 1330; 1330; Issue Date: 02/14/2005; Planning, Programming, Budgeting, and Execution as cited in the FEMA Strategic Plan, Fiscal Years 2008-2013)

Program Proponent: For FEMA purposes, the Program Proponent is the program office or organization that resides in the operational line of authority. The Program Proponent has the immediate authority to decide a course of action or has the authority to recommend a course of action from among alternatives to the next higher organizational level (e.g. region to Headquarters) for approval. The Program Proponent has the authority to establish resource requirements for a proposed action or, in the execution phase, has the authority to direct the use of resources. While the Program Proponent is not normally expected to personally execute and document the environmental planning process, he or she has the lead role and is responsible for initiating the effort and ensuring EHP compliance for program actions. Examples include the Public Assistance Grant Program, the Individuals and Households Program, the various grant programs administered by the Federal Insurance and Mitigation Administration, the various grant programs administered by the Grant Programs Directorate, and the Support Services and Facilities Management Division. (Source: DHS Directive 023-01)

Regional Environmental Officer (REO): The Regional Environmental Officer (REO) fulfills the role of the Environmental Planning Program Manager in each of FEMA's ten regional offices, and is responsible for providing comprehensive regulatory, policy, guidance, scoping, assessment, planning, training, and technical assistance for FEMA Programs and activities to comply with relevant EHP laws, executive orders, and implementing regulations.

Stakeholders: Person, group or organization that has an interest in something; for purposes of FEMA's EHP compliance, stakeholders have an interest because they can affect or be affected by FEMA's actions, objectives and policies. Key stakeholders in the EHP compliance process include grantees and sub-grantees, communities and the general public, and Federal, Regional, Territorial, Tribal and State resource agencies and organizations, among others.

Appendix B: Link to FEMA and DHS Strategic Plans and OEHP Performance Measures

EHP Strategic Goals & Objectives	EHP Performance Metrics	FEMA GOALs					DHS OSEP Goals				
		Lead an integrated approach that strengthens the Nation's ability to address disasters, emergencies, and terrorist events.	Deliver easily accessible and coordinated assistance for all programs	Provide reliable information at the right time for all users	FEMA invests in people and people invest in FEMA to ensure mission success	Build public trust and confidence through performance and stewardship	Develop integrated policies, procedures, and guidance to provide sustainable program management	Establish Department-wide metrics to optimize performance and ensure accountability	Improve program effectiveness through outreach with stakeholders	Sustain program excellence by investing in our personnel	Provide advocacy and oversight to ensure the effective and efficient use of resources
Goal 1 Build Sustainable Capabilities											
1.1 Strengthen EHP Human Capital	% of projects cleared through EHP queues in more than 60 days [by program]; % of EHP cadre at a minimum of Level 3 proficiency; % of Target EHP cadre staffing level onboard; % of projects for which EHP approval is made by program staff; need to develop readiness metric	X	X		X	X				X	X
1.2 Develop an investment and funding support strategy to meet FEMA's EHP compliance goals and Program Metrics.	G3, FY09	X	X	X	X	X		X			X
Goal 2 Strengthen Operational Effectiveness											
2.1 Simplify, standardize and improve the EHP compliance process across all Programs.	% of projects cleared through EHP queues is less than 30 days [by program]; % of projects cleared through EHP queues in more than 60 days [by program]; % of projects that received 1 or more EHP expedited or streamlined reviews. [by law]	X	X	X		X		X	X		X
2.2 Integrate EHP requirements into program goals, development, implementation, and performance	% of projects cleared through EHP queues is less than 30 days [by program]; % of projects cleared through EHP queues in more than 60 days [by program]; % of projects that received 1 or more EHP expedited or streamlined reviews [by law]	X	X	X		X		X	X		X
2.3 Leverage technology in the EHP compliance process.	% of projects cleared through EHP queues is less than 30 days [by program]; % of projects cleared through EHP queues in more than 60 days [by program]; % of projects that received 1 or more EHP expedited or streamlined reviews [by law]. % of projects for which EHP approval is made by program staff; need to develop readiness metric; need to develop CIO/ technology measure	X	X	X		X		X			X
2.4 Evaluate the reliability, consistency, cost-effectiveness, and timeliness of FEMA's EHP compliance.	% of projects cleared through EHP queues in more than 60 days [by program]; % of projects that received 1 or more EHP expedited or streamlined reviews [by law]. % of projects for which EHP approval is made by program staff; need to develop readiness metric; need to develop additional outcome measures (e.g. quality, cost effectiveness)	X	X	X		X		X			X
Goal 3 Strengthen Partnerships											
3.1 Increase awareness of the value of the EHP compliance process across FEMA programs and among stakeholders, in order to foster a sense of ownership of and responsibility for EHP compliance.	% of projects that received 1 or more EHP expedited or streamlined reviews [by law]. % of projects for which EHP approval is made by program staff; need to develop readiness metric; need to develop effectiveness measure	X	X	X		X			X		X
3.2 Improve coordination with Resource Agencies.	% of projects cleared through EHP queues is less than 30 days [by program]; % of projects cleared through EHP queues in more than 60 days [by program]; % of projects that received 1 or more EHP expedited or streamlined reviews [by law]. % of projects for which EHP approval is made by program staff;		X	X		X			X		X
3.3 Develop and implement EHP partnering opportunities to advance the FEMA mission.	Need to develop effectiveness measure	X	X	X		X					X

Appendix C: Summary of Implementation Plans and Priority Strategies

(Estimated Resources, Cost Requirements, & Timeframes)

During the EHP Strategic Planning process, the Steering Committee identified priority strategies that would create the largest gain in progress for the goals of the Plan. These Steering Committee developed detailed implementation plans which include: implementation steps, and by step, outcomes, internal and external players required, estimated contract and travel costs, estimated start and finish dates. Other strategies, not included in this summary, have similar detailed implementation plans with additional costs associated with them. Those details are not included in this summary. **X** under Internal connotes project lead for strategy.

		STRATEGY	Outcome and/or Deliverable	Advisory Committee	OEHP	REO	Pgrm	OCC	OCIO	EMI	OPPA	Human Capital	OSHE	External Affairs	DWF	State/Tribal	USFW	NPS	USFW	NCSHPO	NATHPO	Resource Agencies	Estimated Contract Support Cost	Estimated start	Estimated finish	Duration (months)
GOAL 1	a	Strategy 1.1.1 Identify required EHP capabilities and staffing levels across FEMA necessary to achieve mission	Resource Baseline and Gap Analysis	X	X	X	X	X	X			X			X								$ 38,000	1-Nov-2008	1-Sep-2009	10
	b	Strategy 1.1.2: Develop Human Capital Plan based on FEMA-wide EHP competencies.	HCP with Implementation recommendations	X	X	X	X	X	X	X	X	X			X								$ 85,000	9-Sep-2008	31-Oct-2010	26
	c	Strategy 1.2.1: Develop a business case justifying the need to fund EHP capabilities required to effectively meet our FEMA mission.	Approved budget	X	X	X	X	X	X	X	X	X			X	X	X	X	X	X	X		$ 60,000	1-Oct-2008	1-Mar-2009	5
GOAL 2	d	Strategy 2.1.1: Align FEMA Environmental Regulations/ Management Directives to DHS Management Directives.	Finalized Implementation Plan	X	X	X	X	X	X	X	X	X			X	X	X	X	X	X	X		$ 150,000	1-Nov-2008	1-Jun-2011	31
	e	Strategy 2.1.2: Develop and Implement an EHP Policy Framework	Updated Policies	X	X	X	X	X	X	X	X		X	X	X								$ -	1-Sep-2009	30-Sep-2013	49
	f	Strategy 2.3.1: Institutionalize the Environmental and Historic Preservation Management System (EMIS) as part of a FEMA Enterprise System.	Deployment of EMIS internally and externally	X	X	X	X	X	X	X	X		X	X	X								$ 1,100,000	1-Oct-2009	1-Jun-2011	20
	g	Strategy 2.4.1: Establish performance-based management system for EHP	Set of quality metrics	X	X	X	X	X	X		X				X								$ 20,000	1-May-2008	30-Sep-2009	17
GOAL 3	h	Strategy 3.1.1 Develop and implement EHP Outreach Strategy	Final suite of outreach materials	X	X	X	X	X		X	X				X	X						X	$ 630,000	31-Dec-2008	30-Sep-2013	57
	i	3.1.2 Establish an EHP Advisory Committee at the National level to guide the implementation of the EHP Strategic Plan	EHPAC and a charter established	X	X	X	X	X		X	X		X	X	X								$ -	1-Sep-2008	30-Aug-2013	60
	j	Strategy 3.3.1 Incorporate EHP considerations into planning/preparedness elements	Revised program documents, potential regulatory changes, pilot community workshops, guidance documents	X	X	X	X	X	X	X	X		X	X	X							X	$ 70,000	1-Oct-2010	30-Sep-2013	36
	k	3.3.3: Support FEMA's coordination role under the National Response Framework to coordinate consistent implementation of the EHP requirements and ensure EHP stakeholders regularly participate in these efforts.	Improved operations of response and recovery activities	X	X	X	X	X	X	X	X		X	X	X	X	X	X	X	X	X	X	$ -	1-Oct-2008	1-Sep-2013	59
TOTAL ESTIMATED COSTS & HOURS																										

NOTE: "x" assumes project lead

Estimate on Initial Priority Projects $2,153,000

www.ingramcontent.com/pod-product-compliance
Lightning Source LLC
Chambersburg PA
CBHW080625290526
45790CB00007B/2932